NEW MEXICO STYLE

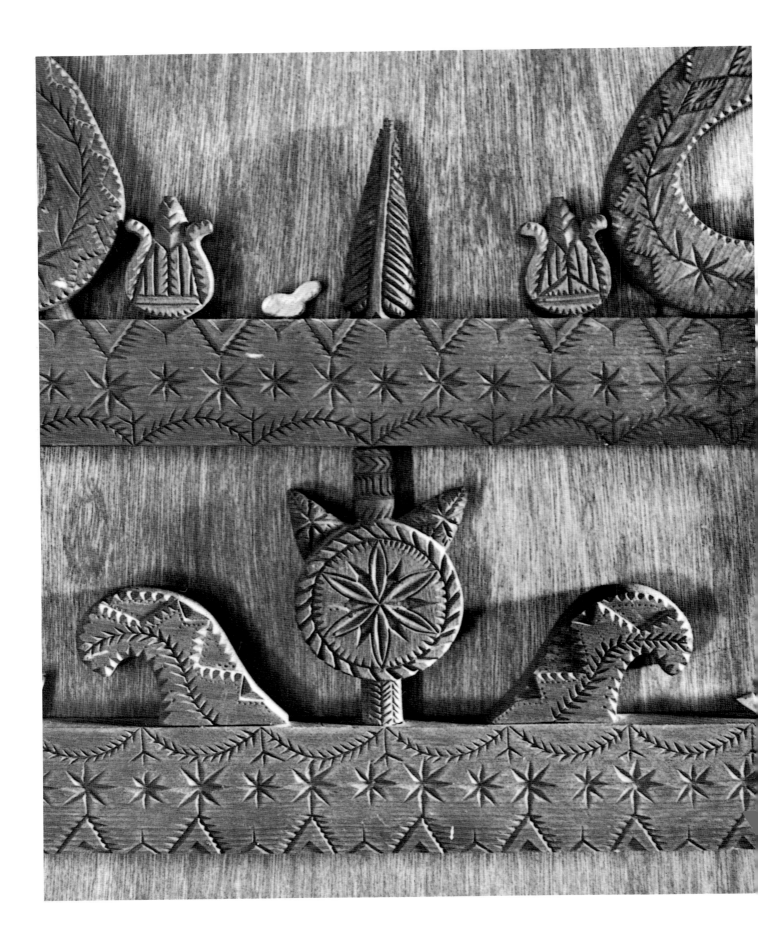

NEW MEXICO STYLE

A Sourcebook of
Traditional Architectural Details

Expanded Edition

Nancy Hunter Warren

Museum of New Mexico Press
Santa Fe

FOR MOTHER

New Mexico Style Expanded Edition is based upon
New Mexico Style, Copyright ©1986 Museum of New Mexico
Press. All photographs ©1986 Nancy Hunter Warren. All
new material ©1995 Nancy Hunter Warren.

Printed in Japan

Front cover: Spanish-Pueblo Revival-style house, Santa Fe.
Frontispiece: Detail of a screen door carved by José Dolores
López (see page 45, left)

Library of Congress Cataloging-in-Publication Data
Warren, Nancy Hunter.
  New Mexico style.

  1. Vernacular architecture—New Mexico.
2. Architecture—New Mexico—Details.   1. Title.
NA730.N38W37   1986   729'.3'09789   86-12424
ISBN 0-89013-279-8

Designed by Daniel Martinez
Expanded Edition design by David Skolkin

MUSEUM OF NEW MEXICO PRESS
Post Office Box 2087
Santa Fe, New Mexico 87504

Contents

A 1920s staircase with cutout designs on the riser boards, Sanat Fe.

Preface to Expanded Edition

During the eight years since publication of *New Mexico Style*, I have discovered and documented many more interior and exterior architectural details. It is still exciting to capture on film an old chip-and-gouged–carved gate or corbel, previously unnoticed or undiscovered, or to happen upon a new home using either traditional architectural elements or a contemporary version of an old Hispanic or Pueblo design.

During these past years, I have had the opportunity to photograph the interiors of several old historic Santa Fe homes, concentrating on fireplaces and *alacenas* which can be considered an integral part of the architectural design, and also on the old tin and iron fixtures which I consider "additions to" both interior and exterior architectural details. And, despite my preference for the abstracting qualities of a good black-and-white photograph, I have been recording in color things for which color is an essential part of their impact.

Additional doors and gates, window treatments, and corbels complete the material new to this edition. Along with some colonial examples, others are valuable additions to the record of decorative work done in New Mexico beginning with the 1920s Revival period and continuing into the present. Many of these photographs were made possible through the generosity of William Field, who gave me free access to one of the most important early homes in Santa Fe.

Sadly, the old examples continue to disappear, either through neglect or simply old age. I have seen fine, old, delicately chip-carved shutters painted over with a dark coat of thick paint, and I

A portal post copied from the old example, Santa Fe.

have watched a wonderful old gate sagging on its hinges—no longer used or cared for. But the inherited New Mexican decorative style is still important to many of today's builders and homeowners, and whether found on a new or remodeled house, it is always a gratifying pleasure to discover a decorative element apparently inspired by the first edition of this book.

Traditional rosette on wooden gate, Santa Fe.

Preface to First Edition

My introduction to Santa Fe was a week's stay at La Fonda Hotel and a rental car that let me lose myself among the city's dirt roads and streets "sin nombre." Immediately, I was caught up in the uniqueness and charm of what I was seeing. Never before had I wandered along narrow winding roads edged with irrigation ditches or seen adobe homes half hidden behind high walls with handmade gates giving each its own flavor. I learned about the special qualities of a town influenced by several different cultures, separate in some ways yet blending together in others. I wanted to live in such a place.

Later, after years of becoming a part of, and seeing more of, this special city, I began to notice other architectural excitements. I found old canales carved with simple designs, a mailbox with a beautiful Taos blue rosette cut from tin surrounding the opening, and windows hand-painted with wonderful designs. My horizons broadened when I began to notice that other towns, such as Albuquerque's Old Town, Taos, and many of the small villages, had similar architectural details. Some of these details were old and weathered; others were new, made to emulate the old, continuing the traditional style.

As a photographer and a lover of folk art, I had no choice but to record these treasures. The old pieces were beginning to disappear—some being replaced with commercial substitutes. But many of the newer pieces were handmade and worthy of recording also.

The creative continuum was apparent. Some pieces were made in imitation of old designs, but others were more modern in feeling.

For three years, I toured northern New Mexico, wandering along main streets and small dirt roads, looking for examples of this folk craft. Finding a new and different example was always exciting and more than made up for the barking dogs and the necessity, now and then, of having to return several times to get a good photograph.

Since this project was developed over such a long period of time, place names were sometimes not recorded—thus, the occasional omission of this information in the photograph captions. Dating the pieces photographed was usually very difficult and therefore not likely to be accurate, so dates have not been included in the captions.

I am sure I have only skimmed the surface. There must be many more handmade doors or corbels hidden away behind other adobe walls. But this is a beginning. I thank Charlene Cerny for suggesting and encouraging the idea of this book; Bobby Byrnes, who often drove while I watched for the next great example; Bob LeMunyon, whose expertise in woodworking and knowledge of technical matters helped me write the captions; and Bill Lumpkins, whose introduction adds an invaluable historical overview to the book.

Nancy Hunter Warren, 1986

Abstract radial design decorating a wooden sign, Taos.

Introduction

The building of homes, especially in rural areas of New Mexico, has always been a do-it-yourself undertaking, resulting in diverse and original works, particularly in the embellishment of architectural details. The skills of New Mexico's many artists and craftsmen have helped foster the idea that if one works within tradition, creativity can flourish, and designs can be freely borrowed and modified. Nancy Hunter Warren's photographs of gates, windows, doors, posts, corbels, railings, canales, coverups, and mailboxes provide a long-needed documentation of the use of folk-craft motifs in exterior architectural details in New Mexico. The clarity of these photographs, in lieu of drawings, captures the charm of simply made things.

The tradition of New Mexico crafts began more than two thousand years ago, as the Indians of the area developed basket making, pottery, and weaving and added decorative elements to their work. However, relatively little is known about decorative exterior details in Pueblo architecture before the arrival of the Spanish. Pit houses were followed by many-roomed apartmentlike units of earth and stone and finally in the seventh to the thirteenth centuries by the great stone cities of northwestern New Mexico. After the thirteenth century, the Pueblo Indians moved south along the Rio Grande, building large multistoried towns of earth and stone with the stepped or "sky-altar" shape still characteristic of pueblos today.

Wetted soil for the structures was shaped by hand along wall lines and allowed to dry; then further layers were added, resulting in walls from four to seven stories high. Pine or fir logs were used to support the roof, with small poles forming the deck for succeeding dirt floors and ultimately for dirt roofs. The structures had no windows, generally no doors (access being gained through holes in the roof), and certainly no mailboxes. There is no evidence of corbels on supporting pillars. We do know that walls were sometimes decorated with paintings and murals, and rocks were sometimes laid in patterns. Pueblo buildings today are usually not decorated on the outside.

In 1598, a small band of some four hundred Spanish settlers, under the command of Oñate, moved north from Mexico along the Rio Grande to a site west of a pueblo that is today called San Juan. From the many elements of their culture, the Spanish brought metal tools, the fireplace, the horno (outdoor beehive oven), and the adobe brick, all of which were adopted by the Indians.

For purposes of defense, Spanish structures consisted of square or rectangular enclosures of adobe, the houses forming one-story walls around an inner patio or plaza with the only access by means of heavy gates. In addition to gates, exterior architectural details used by the Spanish included canales, or spouts, to carry off rain and melting snow; very narrow doors and small windows (a few of the latter glazed with mica), both facing inward for defense purposes; and corbels. Spanish canales, gates, doors, and corbels, as well as window frames, grills, and shutters, were all made of wood.

People decorated those elements as time allowed. Many Spanish design motifs, such as the half shell, the rosette, and the pomegranate, were in fact derived from Roman stone carving, which the Spanish in Spain had translated into wood. The building style changed very little in the Spanish villages and the occasional large haciendas of the Southwest for over two hundred and fifty years, though there undoubtedly were opportunities for individual creativity and whimsy in the use of decorative elements within the design tradition.

Then in the 1820s, pack-mule trains arrived from almost unknown neighbors some eight hundred miles to the east—the Anglo-American traders. These early pack trains brought little more than soft goods and trinkets, however. In the 1830s, the great wagon trains began to arrive in large numbers along what became known as the Santa Fe Trail. Wagon trains brought new tools and a certain number of wood pediments and moldings for windows and doors, based on a modified Greek Revival style, and Anglo carpenters introduced ideas that Spanish carpenters copied and adapted. But very little in the way of building materials, such as ready-made doors with metal hardware, glass for windows, or roofing materials—items that could have improved the buildings—came west along the trail. These had to await the coming of the railroad in the 1880s.

With the railroad came other tools—scroll and band saws, as well as more sophisticated lathes for turning spindles. These tools had a refining effect

1

on furniture and also on interior and exterior architectural details, such as gates, corbels, railings, portal posts, and window grills. Ready-made window sash glazed with glass and doors with metal hardware arrived in large quantities, changing the look of the house, both inside and outside. Houses no longer had to serve as fortresses, and larger windows and doors opened up dark interiors. More and larger single houses began to be built, with encircling yards requiring fences and small garden gates.

The sawmill, which had been introduced in the 1850s, dramatically changed both interior and exterior building systems. The basic wall construction remained sun-dried brick, but local lumber, which had been hand-hewn, became mass-produced, allowing time for more elaborate designs. As soon as brick plants were established in southern Colorado and the railway was extended through New Mexico, brick coping appeared on the tops of walls.

But the most dramatic change to building exteriors came with the introduction of shingles and metal for roofs. This, in turn, introduced the gable, dormer, boxed eaves, and hip roof. The new form of roof was rapidly added to existing roofs, especially in the northern part of the state, where the heavy winter snows destroyed flat roofs. There is no conclusive evidence that either shingles or metal roofing materials arrived ahead of the railroads.

Prior to the turn of the century, turned porch columns and cutout gingerbread for roof and porch trim and finish began to arrive by railroad in rather large amounts, often ordered from catalogs. These exterior details inspired local Spanish craftsmen to create their own versions. Such enrichment is most noticeable in the northern part of New Mexico above Española. Though they are now almost all lost, there were many fine examples of creative adaptation on house exteriors in the villages of Los Lunas and Socorro. In more remote towns, such as Tierra Amarilla and Park View, details like spindles and trim were used with considerable imagination. Spindle rails were sometimes cut in half to make twice as many

Territorial portal posts decorated with Queen Anne-style scrollwork on portal of nineteenth-century house, Socorro.

Traditional northern New Mexico village house with pitched metal roof, Peñasco.

spindles, creating rails half as high, and ready-made elements were sometimes inserted upside down. In larger towns like Santa Fe, where there was more Anglo influence, these details were used in more conventional ways.

When artists from other parts of the country invaded the Taos area in the late 1800s and Santa Fe in the 1920s, a rich creative force was added to the local craft of building. These artists came from sophisticated backgrounds, but they were drawn to the traditional building styles they found in New Mexico. Often aspiring do-it-yourselfers, they bought old abandoned Spanish homes and renovated them, adding decorative painting and carving of their own invention and adapted from other folk-craft traditions to both interiors and exteriors. Stepped-style adobe homes, inspired by the pueblos, were also built, often mixing elements from traditional Pueblo and Spanish architecture. Many examples of these creations can still be seen, particularly in Taos and Santa Fe, and some more recent artists in the area have carried on this tradition.

In the early 1930s, when the state and national economy was at a low ebb, the production of local crafts was given impetus by both the public and the private sectors, resulting in a vigorous crafts revival. The State of New Mexico, in a reorientation of the Department of Vocational Education under the direction of Brice Sewell, expanded traditional Spanish furniture and door making, weaving, pottery, embroidery, tanning, and tinwork. Small schools teaching these crafts were set up throughout the state, and a central outlet for the crafts, The Native Market, was established by the Curtin family in Santa Fe. The schools also provided sales space for the students' work, and in some villages, small markets were established. As trainees felt competent, individual shops were opened, sometimes expanding the training of new workers with an in-shop apprenticeship program.

The National Youth Administration (NYA) enrolled many students in these schools and supplied them with a minimum support salary. In Albuquerque, the NYA occupied a large vacant store building and equipped it with woodworking machines, establishing a large training and production center there. Sponsors, who furnished the lumber, were found in state government agencies, schools, and hospitals; students turned out desks, chairs, cabinets, bookcases, and filing cabinets for them. This project was so successful that the students had soon furnished the sponsors with all their needs, and the project was ended for lack of demand. Then with the onset of war in Europe and a directive from Washington, most of the crafts schools were closed or converted to training centers for the war effort.

During World War I, West Coast industries discovered New Mexico's large pool of skilled workers and offered them wages that drew many craftsmen to that area. Some of the craftsmen stayed in New Mexico, however, and some returned in later years to establish crafts shops. Later, during the Great Depression, private homes and state buildings acquired many more crafts objects. Most of these were not exterior details, though some doors, corbels, and carved spiral posts were made to order for clients. But the quantity of furniture-making, weaving, tinwork, embroidery, tanning, and pottery objects made design details from the Spanish crafts tradition highly visible, and it can be assumed that these served to perpetuate the use of exterior architectural details as well.

With the arrival of counterculture youth in the 1960s and 1970s, yet another Anglo influence affected architectural details in New Mexico. In striving to create or return to a self-sufficient life-style, they became do-it-yourselfers, emulating the building techniques of the Spanish and the Indians. Though initially the results of the young people's experiments were often disastrous, they learned traditional techniques and ultimately added creative elements of their own, such as irregular wall contours and fanciful details on doors, windows, walls, and corbels. These contributions are now accepted as a part of New Mexico style.

The tradition of making do with what is at hand, working creatively within a multicultural tradition, continues today in New Mexico, in all segments of its population. Nancy Hunter Warren's sensitive and comprehensive collection of photographs of exterior architectural details can be used as an inspiring source book for such projects. Architects, builders, remodelers, and handymen can use it as a springboard for their own creativity, further enriching a tradition that is centuries old. For after constructing the essentials, all people feel the need to enhance their work.

Bill Lumpkins

Brick coping defines flat roof on this typical Territorial-style house, Santa Fe.

Vigas and softly contoured adobe walls characterize this Spanish-Pueblo Revival-style house, Santa Fe.

Corbels and Portal Posts

Corbels and beams, carved with simple geometric or floral designs, were the earliest, and often the only, ornamentation found on the otherwise plain seventeenth-century mission churches. Spanish friars began the New Mexican tradition of decorating architectural details by teaching the local Indians woodworking techniques, showing them designs, such as rosette and shell patterns, that were originally based on Spanish Renaissance and Moorish sources. But with time and isolation, and the Indian craftsmen's modification of proportions and feeling, the original Spanish purity of design was diluted. In many cases, the style of New Mexican wood carving became an abstraction of originally complex forms and designs, with many of the primary meanings lost. During these colonial times, woodworking was hampered by the small number of skilled carpenters and the limited variety of tools available; but despite this, beautifully hand-carved corbels decorated the Spanish mission churches. Over the next four centuries, Spanish, Indian, and Anglo carpenters continued to use many of the old styles on homes, as well as on churches, along with new designs brought about by evolving influences from other areas.

The basic function of a corbel is to distribute evenly the weight of heavy roof beams to an adobe wall or a portal post. In some early examples, two corbels and a beam were cut from a single massive piece of wood. Usually, though, each corbel is cut separately and attached to the supporting beam. In more recent years, nonfunctional corbels, such as some used in corners or those made in sections, have been added to support beams for purely decorative reasons.

During the Spanish and Mexican eras, corbels and beams were hand adzed to smooth and roughly shape the wood. The sometimes-intricate silhouette on corbels were cut with saws, and their decoratively carved surfaces were incised and chip carved, often in repetitious patterns. At times, color was added with natural earth dyes. These Spanish-Pueblo wood carving traditions were continued after New Mexico became a territory of the United States in 1846 but on a somewhat lesser scale. Building designs changed gradually as a localized Territorial style based on the eastern Greek Revival fashion adapted itself to frontier folk conditions. With the coming of the railroad in 1879, there was a further influx of architectural styles, such as the Queen Anne-style, overlapping and competing with each other in popularity. In actual practice, many buildings became mixtures of different architectural designs. In the early 1900s the decorating of corbels and beams revived in popularity as part of a Spanish-Pueblo revival and was encouraged by artists who had moved into the area today, this decoration remains a vital part of many New Mexican homes.

Portal posts, on which corbels rest, evolved from the plain log supports of the colonial period to the creative spiral and commercially turned designs of the early twentieth century. Perhaps, the most interesting examples are the heavy, square, mill-cut posts that were decorated by hand, using chisels and a saw. Many effective designs were made with only a few simple tools and some paint to accentuate the cutout motifs. Other popular designs for portal supports consisted of variations on diagonal channeling carved around the post—usually finished with paint or clear varnish. Post designs like these, while found in other areas of New Mexico, were particularly popular in the small northern mountain villages.

Contemporary hand-carved corbel and beam, featuring a concave rosette, Pecos National Monument.

Above, old and weathered corbel probably shaped with adze and chisel, Chimayó. Below, modern example of a simply designed corbel, Santa Fe.

bove, *nicely carved, unadorned corbel and beam, San Ildefonso Pueblo.* **Below,** *recent adaptation of an undecorated corbel, Santa Fe.*

bove, corbel and beam decorated with rows of bullet carving. **Below**, *plain corbel supporting a rough chip-carved square beam, Taos.*

Above, *unusual double corbel with etched star and floral designs, Abiquiu.* **Below,** *corbel with designs chiseled in relief, along with gouge cuts and bullet carving, Abiquiu.*

16

bove, *old church corbel built up of layers of heavy timber, Santa Cruz.* **Below,** *series of painted steps and curves forming an unusual church* *rbel, Laguna Pueblo.*

17

Tongue and groove boards nailed to upper beam to form a decorative false corbel, Alcalde.

Above **left and right,** *mail-order Queen Anne-style gingerbread brackets brought from the East by the railroad:* **left,** *Los Ojos;* **right,** *Santa Fe.* **Below left and right,** *locally made copies of imported Queen Anne-style brackets:* **left,** *Santa Fe;* **right,** *Cleveland.*

Above, *modern corner corbel with minimal carving, supported by two tapered posts, Picurís Pueblo.* Below, *corner corbel with a pseudo-adzed facing, Taos.*

bove, *double-ended corbel supporting the beam at a lap joint, Santa Fe.* **Below,** *vigas, extending over a portal and supported by beam and* *ouble-ended corbel, Santa Fe.*

Above, *double-ended corbel with incised geometric designs, Santa Fe.* Below, *minimally carved corbel supporting a bullet-carved beam, Dixon.*

Above, pseudo-corbels nailed to supporting post for decorative effect, Santa Fe. **Below,** *old paint and a unique design highlighting a rustic double-ended corbel, Santa Fe.*

Opposite page, above: *double-ended corbel supporting dovetailed adzed beam to form a strong juncture, Taos;* middle, *simple corbel with scalloped profile, Santa Fe;* below, *double-ended corbel that is structurally weak because of its center lap joint, Taos.*

Above, *unusual modern adaptation of a corbel, Taos.*

Above, *old, roughly cut corbel, Santa Fe.* Below, *hand-hewn corbel with incised designs along with unusual carving on the underside.*

26

Left, *square portal post chip carved along a single chamfered edge,*
Santa Fe.

Opposite page, top left and right, *geometric patterns created*
by simple saw and chisel cuts for square posts: **top left,** *Peñasco;* **top**
right, *El Valle.* **Bottom left,** *rough-cut boards separated by blocks to*
make an inexpensive portal post, with color highlighting the different
sections, El Valle. **Bottom right,** *notched board creating an unusual*
portal post.

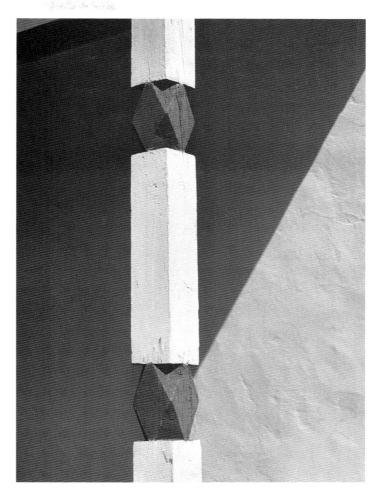

Left, *square post decorated with cruciform design defined by saw-cut grooves, Peñasco.*

Opposite page, left, *old lathe-turned pillar, possibly factory-made, a likely inspiration for local design variations, Contreras.* **Opposite page, right,** *brightly painted geometric designs on a square pillar, Santa Fe.*

Doors

Wooden doors were first introduced into New Mexico by the Spanish colonists for mission churches and the more well-to-do homes. Previously, blankets, skins, or woven reed mats were used to keep the cold out of dwellings. A few examples of old wooden exterior doors have been found in churches and in the remains of some homesteads. These heavy doors generally lacked metal hinges, relying instead on wooden pintles, an arrangement that allowed the doors to rotate. They were made of from six to eight hand-hewn panels fastened together by a mortise and tenon frame. Doors in the early days were usually quite small—often only two feet wide and four to five feet high. Most were undecorated, but a few Spanish friars taught Indians carving techniques in order to ornament church doors and corbels. Many of the ordinary homes had their main doors decorated in a similar manner.

With the arrival of the railroad in the late nineteenth century, New Mexico architecture began to change drastically. Eastern influences, in design, new tools, and mill-sawn lumber, opened the way for a flood of diverse architectural styles. Distinctive doors became a trademark of the period. The true frame and panel doors from colonial times were replaced by doors made of strips of hand-planed molding nailed onto milled lumber boards. The native carpenters became skilled at creating new and interesting two-ply patterns. Doors and door casings were often decorated with elaborate designs. Pedimented lintels over doors and windows are another trademark of this period. Beginning as simple design elements, the lintels became increasingly complex with more and more decorative moldings added.

An adjunct to the architecture of the territorial period is a folk-art style that began toward the end of the nineteenth century in the isolated mountain villages of Truchas, Los Luceros, Rodarte, Llano,

Chacon, and Peñasco. Cut off from distant commercial sources, the local carpenters began to construct beautiful doors for their adobe farmhouses. Innocent of direct prototypes, they elaborated and modified old classical styles, using their own motif variations. With sufficient quantities of sawn lumber and good tools available, they integrated hand-cut door moldings with fanciful outlines cut with a jigsaw. Even though these doors are known as Peñasco doors, the designs vary from village to village, each having a unique set of forms. The doors are made by combining rectangular panels with panels of looping ogee forms and integrating fanciful shapes, such as stars, crosses, diamonds, and squares, often painted in contrasting colors. This tradition lasted only through isolation. After World War I, new roads and motorized vehicles allowed manufactured doors to be brought into these remote villages.

Sometime after the 1920s, José Dolores López, a Córdova wood-carver, began to make wooden screen door frames for homes in Santa Fe and elsewhere in New Mexico. These highly decorative doors incorporated intricate chip-carving techniques, as well as carved names and humorous figures of trees, birds, and animals. These seldom-seen doors are delightful examples of creativity in the folk arts.

Beginning in the early 1900s, the Spanish-Pueblo Revival style of architecture was adopted by many of the artists living in the Santa Fe and Taos areas. Their artistic inclinations extended to decorating many of the small architectural details of their homes. Doors, as well as architectural details, were carved and painted in unique ways, reflecting American ideas, as well as adapting traditional Pueblo and Spanish motifs.

Old door of applied wood in diamond and square patterns, San Augustine.

Left, *modern plank door set in a diamond pattern, Taos.* Right, *simple church door of rough-cut applied lumber, Arroyo Seco.*

Left, *contemporary door with sunburst design set in an old adobe frame, Dixon.* **Right,** *cruciform design made with applied molding and diagonal boards in lower panel, Arroyo Hondo.*

Peñasco doors of applied designs and decorative molding: **left**, Santa Fe; **right**, Peñasco.

Top Left, *an early wood-plank door with applied wood elements. Lead roofing nails and chip carving are used as additional decoration, Santa Fe.* Top Right, *section of an old morada door made from hand-finished planks. Originally painted a deep red, it was later over painted with white pigment. The wooden latch is hand carved, Arroyo Hondo.* Above, *small wood-paneled door, once used as a pass-through for ice delivery. The heart ia a recent addition, Santa Fe.*

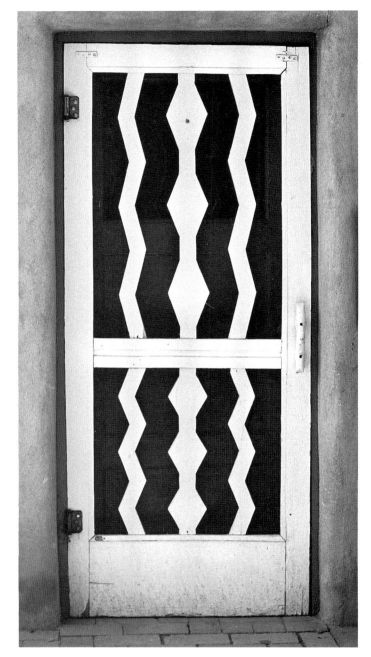

Above left, *stock Queen Anne-style screen door shipped from the East around 1900, Santa Fe.* **Below left,** *local copy of Queen Anne-style factory-made screen door set in a painted adobe doorway, Taos.* **Above,** *contemporary screen door with simple zigzag cutouts, Albuquerque.*

Opposite page, *local craftsman's version of a Territorial doorway, using stock window sash.*

Decoratively applied lengths of wood enhancing double garage doors, which have been widened by the addition of two flanking boards, Santa Fe.

Applied diamond and rosette designs enhancing double garage doors, Santa Fe.

Above, *short lengths of milled lumber applied to plywood backing to create an interesting geometric design on double doors, Taos.* Middle, *old double garage doors with random-width horizontal boards, Santa Fe.* Below, *garage doors made of rustic boards, Taos.*

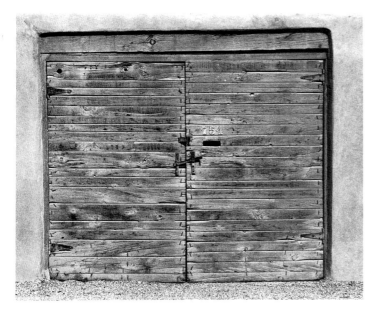

Above, *garage door with applied Zia symbol, Taos.* Below, *modern garage door painted with Pueblo motifs, Taos.*

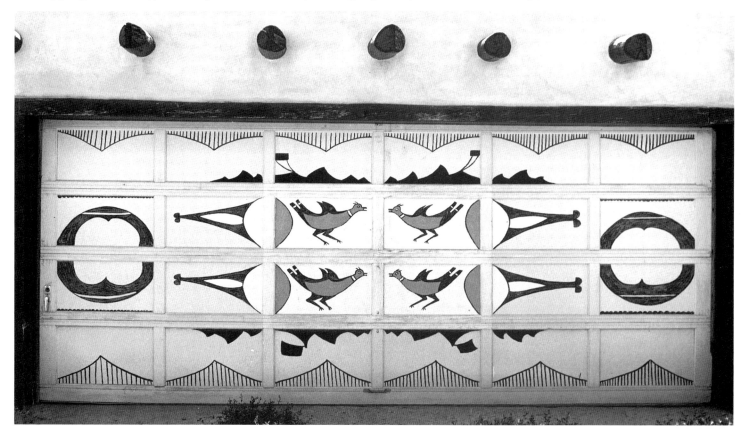

New Mexico Style in Color

The colors used to paint the decorative details on New Mexico's architecture seem to spring from the colors of the environment: the intense blue of the sky, the reds found in a winter sunset or a red chili *ristra*, the yellow seen in autumn's chamisa and cottonwood trees, and the more subtle colors of the desert. These have become a part of us, creating a love of color that often finds expression in the material world.

Very little is known about the availability of paint during the early colonial years, but, with few exceptions, wood surfaces were apparently left bare or coated with a protective varnish made from pine resin. It is well documented that by the late eighteenth century, village *santeros*, who had begun making *bultos* and *retablos* for the churches, were using water-soluble pigments, made from locally available sources, to paint their religious images. It seems likely that some furniture and architectural features were painted during this period, but it wasn't until after the 1880s, when commercially made paints became available, that there was a more widespread decorative use of paint. During the Spanish-Pueblo Revival period of the 1920s and 1930s, which was the beginning of what we know today as "Santa Fe Style," the use of bright colors on architectural details blossomed. Still, not all gates or corbels are painted. Some are left natural, allowing the beauty of the wood or a carved design to dominate. Color is used selectively. It does not overwhelm but rather adds a touch of nature's colors to what would otherwise be a bland adobe cityscape.

Many different kinds of paint are used on today's architectural features. For exteriors, a weather-resistant oil-base house paint is popular. Interior designs use anything from a water-soluble tempera or an artist's oil paint to the same house paint used outside.

Very few of today's interesting architectural details are commercially made. Individual craftsmen still design, build, and decorate most of them, and it is this hand-crafted look that is appealing and keeps the tradition alive.

Left, *the curve of the arched wooden gate complements the arch in the adobe wall, Santa Fe.* Right, *decorative tiles over a simple gate.*

Above, *an old, sagging double gate adds a touch of charm to this Santa Fe home, Santa Fe.* **Right,** *a simple plank gate is enhanced by the hand-painted Pueblo designs, Taos.*

Left, *faded blue grill with traditional cutout design, Santa Fe.* **Right,** *a detail of an iron window grill showing a green copper flower and a black spider, Taos.*

Above, *a weathered double corbel, supported by a square post, Taos.*
Right, *old portal post with four simple notches creating a cruciform design, Peñasco.*

Left, *an early, elaborately carved square post capped by bold geometric elements, Santa Fe.* **Right,** *color and a simple design give interest to this portal post, Vadito.*

Top left, *a recent window topped with a deeply carved shell design, Albuquerque.* Top right, *An interesting combination of a colorful window screen and a projecting stovepipe, Albuquerque.* Left, *territorial-style window frame with brightly stenciled patterns, Taos.* Above, *a simple red window is complemented by the purple flowers of an old wisteria tree, Santa Fe.*

Top left, *contemporary batten-and-board shutters with cutout heart designs, Ranchos de Taos.* Above, *a stepped design created by opposing paint colors is apparent in these closed shutters, Santa Fe.* Left, *narrow single-board shutter built into an adobe wall, Santa Fe.*

Windows

Windows in colonial New Mexico were small, barred with wooden gratings, and covered with heavy wooden shutters because of the need for defense against Indians and protection from the elements. Sheets of translucent mica or selenite were sometimes used between the bars to admit light while closing off cold air. Oiled paper, cloth, or rawhide soaked in grease were also used for the same purpose. An ordinary seventeenth- or eighteenth-century homestead might have had windows facing only the protected inner courtyard, but if there were windows on an outside wall, they would have been heavily barred and shuttered.

The coming of the railroad brought new architectural styles and factory-made building materials, such as hardware and clear window glass, into the territory from the East. Because of the availability of these products and new design ideas, windows became larger and more decorative. As window grills and shutters were no longer needed for defense, they became more elaborate and were mainly used for decoration. Fancy iron window grills came from Mexico in the early 1900s, and locally carved wooden grills of myriad designs also became popular. Often, the grills had a utilitarian purpose as well; for instance, wooden slats of zigzag design were sometimes used to keep birds and chickens from flying into the house.

The late territorial period saw louvered, paneled and carved shutters added to many buildings for decoration, and curved or triangular designs were used to embellish areas above doors and windows. In lieu of curtains, tissue paper was often cut out and elaborately folded by Spanish women to imitate lace, or they painted curtains and other designs on glass windows. Some small churches painted colorful imitation stained glass on windowpanes.

Today, many of these old and valued traditions are continued, but often using commercial substitutes. The mass-produced grills and shutters that have become common on many newer buildings cannot compare with the charm and individuality of earlier handcrafted examples.

New Mexican adaptation of a Greek Revival window, Arroyo Hondo.

70

Window with Moorish-influenced arches and turned columns, Santa Fe.

Queen Anne-style window shipped from the East, Los Ojos.

Above left, *window accented by Pueblo rain cloud design, Tesuque Pueblo.* **Above right,** *Queen Anne-style window from the East, Los Ojos.* **Left,** *window frame reminiscent of the crafts revival style of the 1930s, Taos.*

Wooden window grills.

Wooden window grills: **opposite above,** *Taos;* **middle left,** *Santa Fe;* **middle right,** *Santa Fe;* **below left,** *Nambe;* **below right,** *Santa Fe.*

Right, *wooden window grill, Albuquerque.*

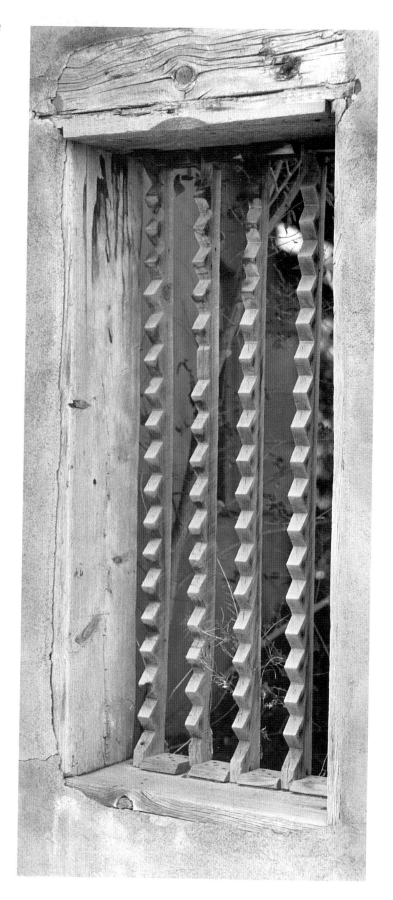

Wooden window grills: **opposite above,** *Santa Fe;* **opposite below,**
Velarde; **right,** *Santa Fe;* **below left,** *Albuquerque;* **below right,**
Santa Fe.

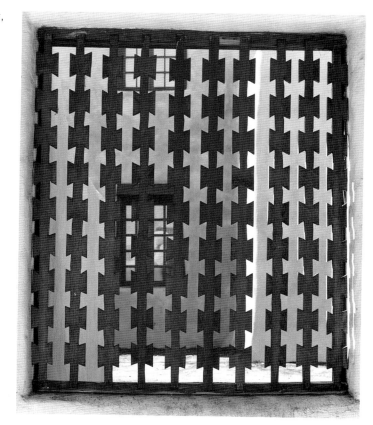

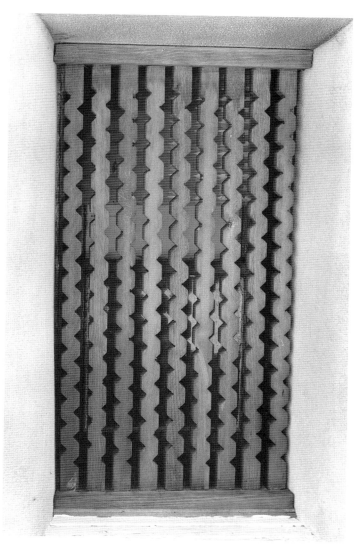

Above, *window grill with turned spindles and capped with a flower and shell crest, Santa Fe.* Below, *freely cut splats set in a simple wooden frame, Santa Fe.*

Old wooden grill with an arched design set into an adobe wall, Santa Fe.

Weathered window grill composed of cutout and pierced slats, Santa Fe.

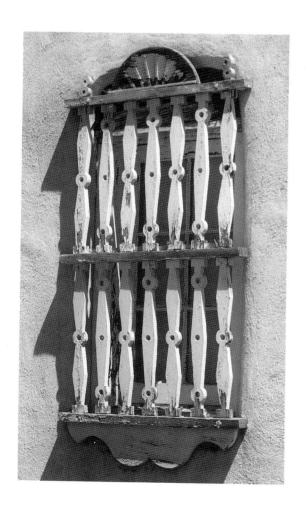

Wooden window grills: **above left**, *Bernardo;* **above right**, *Dixon;* **left**, *Santa Fe.*

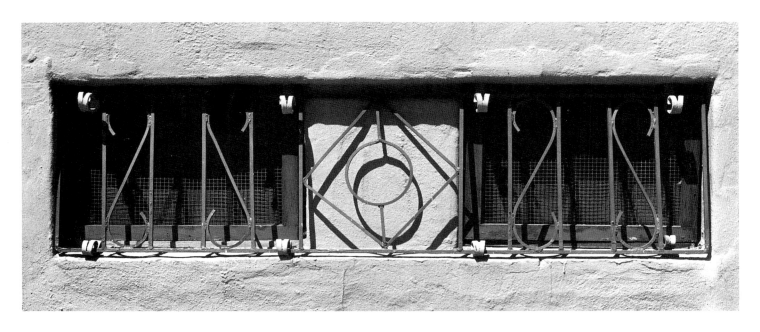

Both old and new metal window grills can be found. They incorporate abstract designs, as well as heart shapes, old Mexican wrought iron, and a Pueblo Indian design. The work includes forging, welding, and split and collared pieces. Note: For safety in fires, window grills should always be capable of opening from the inside out.

Previous page, *Santa Fe;* **above,** *Santa Fe;* **below left,** *San Ildefonso Pueblo;* **below right,** *Santa Fe.*

Above left, above right, left, and following page, *metal window grills, Santa Fe.*

Recent molded-stucco free-form window trim and metal window grill, Albuquerque.

Fireplaces

Perhaps the most interesting example of interior New Mexican architecture is the fireplace. Built with adobe bricks covered with hand-applied plaster, it is usually the focal point of a room, offering heat for warmth and cooking. The plastic nature of the materials used in its construction lends itself to creative differences in shape and decorative details.

The traditional colonial fireplace, known as a *fogón*, was usually built in the corner of a room. The basic shape was simple in design. It had an elliptical opening with a low hearth. The flue was either square or rounded, and it had a small, shallow firebox necessitating short logs that stood on end to burn. Because it produced a large amount of heat from only a few burning logs, it was economical to use.

There have been many variations on the basic corner design which has been expanded and reshaped to conform to specific needs and individual tastes. When placed against a flat wall, a low parapet, or *paredcito*, was constructed at right angles to the wall, creating an artificial corner for the hearth. The short wall also served as a heat sink and to deflect drafts.

In the colonial kitchen, where space was needed for cooking, a larger fireplace was built. The *fogón de campana* had a large bell-shaped hood with a bigger opening and an extended hearth to accommodate cooking pots and to catch any sparks from the fire. One variation of the hooded, bell-shaped fireplace had separate cooking hearths created by two arches supported in the center by a rounded pier.

Another interesting example of colonial design was known as the "shepherd's fireplace." Usually built in a corner of the kitchen, one version can be described as a large hooded fireplace with one side of the vertically sloping hood extending to form a long pole and plastered shelf supported by upright posts. Heat from the fire made the shelf a warm place to sleep on. The open area below was used for food preparation or for keeping the pots warm.

These early corner fireplaces have served as prototypes for those built during and since the Revival period. Some are faithful copies of the original examples, but there are many variations on these designs as changes in size and the addition of mantels, *nichos*, sculptured walls, or painted Southwest designs express individual preferences. But the small, simple colonial fireplace with its perfect proportions has a basic beauty all its own.

A reconstruction of an unusual early village kitchen fireplace. The tall opening, which resembles an inverted V, is edged with a contrasting pigment wash. The massive beam is useful for drying herbs. To the left is an extended adobe work surface, Santa Fe.

An early 1920s kitchen fireplace with large hearth. The hood was made with plastered-over cedar branches, leaving part of the wood exposed, Santa Fe.

Recent corner fireplace with a raised sandstone hearth and a wood storage area below, Santa Fe.

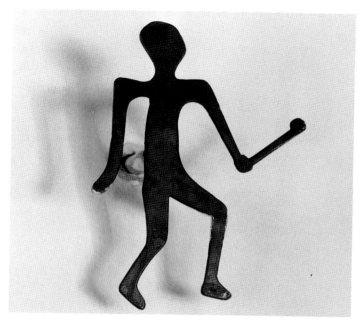

Top left and right, *corner hooded fireplace with an interesting handmade iron damper handle, Santa Fe.* Bottom. *small traditional corner fireplace with stenciled designs, Santa Fe.*

Above, a hooded corner fireplace with a "shepherd's bed" extension made in the late 1920s. The richly decorated wood frame was salvaged from an older building, Santa Fe. Left, old country adobe fireplace with white scalloped trim, Santa Fe.

Top Left, *small corner fireplace with square chimney box, northern New Mexico.* **Top Right,** *kiva fireplace with brass Mimbres designs applied to the fire screen, Santa Fe.* **Left,** *basic unadorned corner fireplace, Santa Fe.* **Above,** *an early bell-shaped fireplace with two openings, originally intended for separate cooking areas. The raised hearth was installed in the 1970s to narrow the air intake for a better draw, Santa Fe.*

Above, *an old restored corner fireplace is made by placing a short parapet at right angles to the wall, Santa Fe.* Below left, *a corner fireplace, with a two-tiered mantel and an attached banco, Santa Fe.* Below right, *early wall fireplace with interesting sculptural qualities, Taos.*

Above, *an old bell-shaped corner fireplace with an unusually large opening and hearth, probably intended for cooking as well as heating, Arroyo Hondo.* Below, *recent corner fireplace with red brick hearth and a massive mantel beam, Santa Fe.* Below right, *a nicely proportioned fireplace with a decorative iron fireplace tool holder, Santa Fe.*

Alacenas

The *alacena*, which can be considered either as furniture or as a part of the architecture, is a recessed wall cupboard that can be found today in both Indian pueblos and Spanish Revival homes. In New Mexico it originated in the colonial period home where storage space was limited. Adobe walls, which varied in thickness from ten inches to more than three feet, allowed for a hollowed-out space that could accommodate a wooden frame, usually with two or three shelves attached. The frame was essentially held in place by the adobe building itself. Pintle-hinged doors fit into the wood frame that was embedded in the wall, eliminating the need for metal hinges. Other doors were attached to their frames with small hand-wrought eyelet hinges. These early doors were often elegantly plain, with only restrained chip carvings to relieve the bare wood. Other, later examples are masterpieces of decorative design, using colorful paint and cutout splats along with the traditional chip-and-gouge carvings.

Sometimes associated with the early *alacenas* were secret compartments masked by an adobe facade and reached only by a sliding wood shelf inside the cupboard. This intriguing feature is adopted in some contemporary homes today.

One *alacena* from the Revival period was custom designed, with three doors dividing the interior space into a bar and glass storage areas. During this same period, old wood panels were often salvaged from eighteenth- and nineteenth-century Spanish or Pueblo ruins and reused to make unusual antique doors for the cupboards.

Old frame-paneled alacena set with pintle hinges, Santa Fe.

Above left and right, *an unusual use of the alacena concept. The double and single doors arrange the interior space to make it useful for serving and storage use, Santa Fe.* Left, *double-door alacena combining zigzag and carved panels, Santa Fe.*

106

Above left, *irregular zigzag cutouts set in a framed double-door alacena, Santa Fe.* Above right, *an early single-panel door utilizing the whirling log motif along with other lightly chiseled designs, Santa Fe.* Left, *antique colonial panel with bold chip carving reused as an alacena door in a 1920s house, Santa Fe.*

Tin and Iron Decorative Details

Decorative tinwork has a long history in New Mexico. During the early nineteenth century, a limited number of tin objects made in Mexico were imported into the territory, but it wasn't until 1846 that New Mexican artisans began making their own decorative tinworks. The opportunity and the impetus for this came when the United States Army began shipping in large tin containers of food and other supplies. The local Hispanic craftsmen, recognizing the discarded cans as the basic material they needed, salvaged the commercially made containers and began creating their own tin designs. These early pieces can often be recognized by remnants of an old lithographed label or an embossed patent marking left on the back side of a tin *nicho* or candle sconce. During this period, the New Mexican artisans, who worked both singly and in group workshops, produced a wide variety of stamped and embossed tinwork, primarily religious pieces, using the discarded army tin containers.

After 1900, handmade tinwork declined in popularity as less expensive factory-made pieces were brought in by the railroad. But new interest in hand-crafted tin developed after the Revival movement in the 1920s and 1930s, partly in response to Anglo artists and collectors who recognized the artistic merits of the work. Using newly available sheet tin, the tinsmiths found new markets for their work, not only for the religious objects but also for electrified sconces, *nichos*, and chandeliers, along with switch plates, mirror frames, and other secular pieces.

The decorative tinwork illustrated here ranges from an early *nicho* that once may have held a small *santo* or religious print, but is now wired for a light bulb, to a more recent switch plate with unique stamped designs made by the homeowner.

Colonial New Mexico did not produce iron naturally, and since only small amounts were imported from Spain and Mexico, iron objects were scarce and highly prized. The local blacksmiths reworked worn-out iron objects when possible, but locally made decorative ironwork was unknown. When possible, other materials were used as substitutes, such as the rawhide door pulls used in place of iron latches.

In the nineteenth century, discarded Conestoga wagon wheels provided an important source of iron to the New Mexico blacksmiths, and the coming of the railroad in 1879 brought needed tools and raw material to the once-isolated people. By the 1930s, as part of the Spanish Revival movement, classes in blacksmithing were being offered to local craftsmen. Their products were sold in the Native Market, a sales outlet supported by Anglo-Americans. Among the crafts offered were tin light fixtures, along with iron locks, hinges, and door latches. The latches shown here are from that period. All are handwrought and were often made for a specific house, state building, or church, as well as for the market.

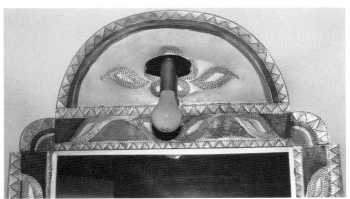

This page and next, *lighting fixtures of punched and cutout tin, Santa Fe.*

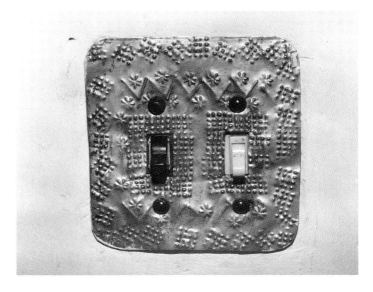

Decorative punched tin switch plates, Santa Fe.

111

Opposite page and left, *old hand-forged door latches, Santa Fe.* Below right, *old door latch, Taos Pueblo.*

113

Canales

Roof drains, or canales, serve to direct the flow of collected rainwater from a flat roof to the ground. The drain projects through a parapet, which serves as a windbreak, carrying the water clear of adobe walls, often onto a splash stone, which diffuses the force of the water.

The earliest examples of canales in New Mexico were made from split logs, hollowed out and lined with galvanized tin to protect the wood from mois- ture. When mill-sawn boards became available, a three-sided box lined with galvanized sheet metal was constructed to form a channel for the water.

Some New Mexicans began decorating their ca- nales. Many of these utilitarian drains have curved or zigzag designs cut along their edges, while others have been incised with simple lines or have been hand carved with rosettes and other designs. In a few instances, plain wood or metal canales have sup- ports of decoratively cut wooden corbels or braces.

Metal canal supported by carved wooden base, Santa Fe.

Above, *scalloped edges adding interest to an old tin-lined canal, Taos.*
Left, *a basic canal style: a split and hollowed log lined with tin, Santa Fe.*

Above, *old wooden canal with incised lines forming a diamond pattern, Santa Fe.* **Below,** *old weathered canal with gently rounded design, Taos.*

Left, *hand-cut zigzag design on bottom edge of wooden canal, Santa*
Below, *wooden canal decorated with step design, Santa Fe.*

Opposite page, *new canales made of rough-cut lumber, Albuquerque.*

119

120

Coverups, Railings, and Mailboxes

The popularity of handcrafted items added a quality that became a part of Spanish-Pueblo Revival style in the 1920s and 1930s. Exuberance of style was encouraged in the decorative treatment of many private homes and public buildings. Even today, this love of craft extends to ways of making a necessary utilitarian object more pleasing to the eye. Simple and unique handmade coverups have been devised to hide eyesores, from gas meters to garbage cans.

Wooden railings, in one form or another, have been used in and on New Mexico buildings since the colonial period. They are found on porches and balconies and as altar rails in many small New Mexican churches. Balconies, while known in the earlier periods, became especially popular during territorial days. The rail supports for these architectural features range from plain boards to scroll-cut pickets to elabora cutouts. As new tools and mill-sawn lumber becam available, designs became more complex and u usual. During the late nineteenth century, it becan fashionable to buy factory-produced railings ar other trim from catalogs, but more often, these de orative additions have been designed and fashione by local craftsmen.

The ordinary mailbox has been creatively recesse into adobe walls, with colorful Mexican tile or painted tin rosette surrounding the mail slot. In son cases, the entire mailbox has been handcrafted wi Spanish designs in wood. In other cases, corbels a used for mailbox bases. Each of these objects is fine example of creativity, something to be valu and preserved in this age of mass production.

rap lumber serving as a coverup for trash cans, Santa Fe.

Above left, *three slats cut from one board, making an attractive coverup for an electric meter, Santa Fe.* **Above right,** *series of simply cut slats and dowels, covering a gas meter, Santa Fe.* **Left,** *an old iron wheel set into an adobe wall, disguising a gas meter, Alcalde.*

Decorative railings are found in churches and on porches, as well as around balconies. Made of milled lumber, the railings usually incorporate repetitious designs cut with saws and often pierced with drill holes. The space between the cutout slats creates a negative counterpart design.

Opposite page: above, *Talpa;* **below,** *Taos.*

125

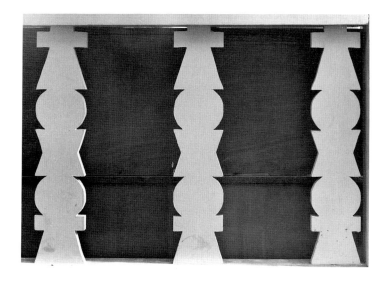

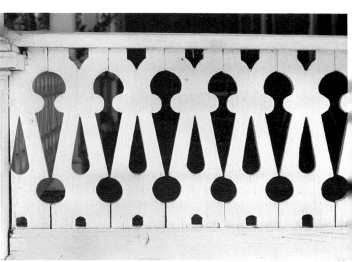

Railings: **above left and above right,** *Santa Fe;* **below left,** *Los Ojos;* **below right,** *Santa Fe.*

126

Railings: **above,** *Taos;* **middle,** *Manuelitas;* **below,** *Córdova.*

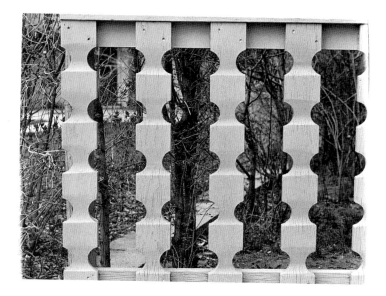

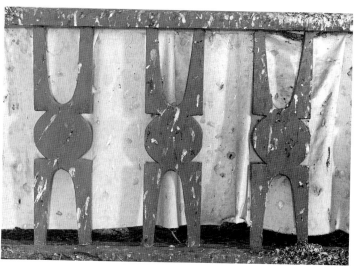

Above and middle left, *Mexican tiles accenting mailbox openings, Santa Fe.* **Below left,** *router-carved mailbox with iron hinges, set in an adobe wall, Santa Fe.* **Above,** *chip-carved mailbox used as part of porch balustrade, Santa Fe.*

ove, *old tin mailbox door with scalloped cresting set into adobe, Santa Fe.* **Below,** *hand-carved wooden rosette set in plaster, serving as a letter* *, Santa Fe.*

129

opposite page: above left, *contemporary communal mailbox highlighted with carved shell designs, Albuquerque. Commercial metal mailboxes* *ting on decorative corbel-like supports,* above right and below left, *Santa Fe;* below right, *Albuquerque.*

ove, freestanding wooden mailbox decorated with a hand-carved rosette design, Santa Fe.

Gates

Early haciendas had little need for garden gates. For defense reasons, these large homes were usually built around enclosed patios, providing some safety from Indian attack. The only opening was the zaguán, a covered passageway with heavy protective doors leading from the outside into the inner courtyard. These large double doors were wide enough to allow the passage of ox carts or farm wagons and were often the only opening in the home's external wall. Cut into one of the large doors was a small gate for pedestrian use. Although few of the old zaguán pedestrian gates still exist, it is evident from the remaining examples that some were cut with a decorated curvilinear top edge.

After the turn of the century, new American immigrants, who were used to gardens surrounding their homes, built adobe or wooden walls to enclose their yards, adding wooden gates, either plain or decorated with carved or painted Indian and Spanish motifs. When available, discarded short doors from houses of the colonial period were salvaged and reused as garden gates. Wrought-iron gates became popular in the early 1900s. Many of these were imported from Mexico, while others were handcrafted in New Mexico. Some of the earliest iron gates reproduced Spanish patterns, but in recent years, the ironworker has begun to create his own design. Wooden garden gates, which have probably been the most popular decorative architectural element northern New Mexico during this century, are now a mixture of old, weathered styles and newer, more modern designs, adding to the uniqueness of today architectural look.

Modern gate of rough-cut lumber tapering from bottom to top, Albuquerque.

133

Left, *gate of rough-cut lumber and hand-carved spindles, Santa Fe.* Right, *old chip-carved gate with pintle hinges, Santa Fe.*

Opposite page, *mitered frame surrounding panels with design elements reminiscent of those found on old New Mexican furniture, Santa Fe.*

135

Above left, *unusual gate with raised panels, a mitered inset, and a unique cutout design, Taos.* **Above right,** *zigzag cutouts adding interest to a paneled gate, Albuquerque.* **Below left,** *old and weathered gate with raised panels and a unique cutout variation of the rosette pattern, Albuquerque.* **Below right,** *old gate with gingerbread design cutouts, Santa Fe.*

Opposite page, *old wooden gate beneath hand-adzed corbel and lintel, Santa Fe.*

Above left, *old gate with two different cutout patterns, Santa Fe.* **Above right,** *arched gate with diamond-shaped cutouts, Alcalde.* **Below left,* *two-sectioned arched gate set into an adobe wall, Taos.* **Below right,** *contemporary gate with a tile-embedded arch, Santa Fe.*

Opposite page, *old iron transom capping a beautifully made narrow gate with raised decorated panels, Santa Fe.*

Above left, *gate with raised panels and handwrought latch, Santa Fe.* **Above right,** *simple three-board arched gate with small cutout opening, Santa Fe.* **Below left,** *patio gate of rough-cut lumber with decorative cresting made by a series of drilled holes and saw cuts, Santa Fe.* **Below right,** *gate made in the tradition of the Peñasco doors, Santa Fe.*

Opposite page, *new gate made with raised panels and the traditional shell design, Santa Fe.*

140

Above left, *recent gate of traditional Spanish design elements, Albuquerque.* **Above right,** *old gate with panels of hand-carved rosettes surrounded by chip carving and topped with a shell pattern—traditional Spanish Colonial designs, Albuquerque.* **Left,** *gate carved one of the early Santa Fe painters, probably in the 1930s, combining traditional Spanish paneling and shell design with Indian dance figure in bas-relief, Santa Fe.*

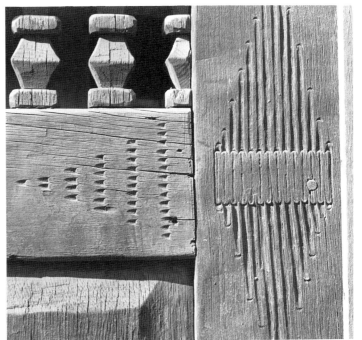

*ove, beautifully carved gate with traditional rosette and shell
igns, along with carved spiral posts, Taos.* **Above right,** *detail from
old chip-carved gate—other examples of this type of chip carving
nd on early New Mexican furniture, Santa Fe.* **Below right,** *gate
ail showing a bold style of chip carving, Santa Fe.*

143

Above left, *old gate made with rough boards decorated with a molding plane and simple cutout designs, Santa Fe.* **Above right,** *recent gate with a sunburst design made of separate boards, Santa Fe.* **Below left,** *modern paneled gate with scroll-like design along the top, Taos.* **Below right,** *boldly designed gate created with incised lines and paint, Taos.*

Board and batten gate enlivened by geometric cutouts, Santa Fe.

Above left, *old paneled gate with shallow chip carving and hand-decorated hinges beneath an arch of corbels and beam, Albuquerque.* **Above right,** *rough-cut lumber with geometric cutouts and hand-hammered hinges, creating an unusual gate, Albuquerque.* **Below left,** *gate made from discarded pieces of an old campo santo marker, Santa Fe.* **Below right,** *interesting gate made with six serrated boards, Albuquerque.*

Geometric cutouts enhancing a paneled gate, Taos.

Above left, *arched gate of milled lumber painted with Pueblo Indian designs, Taos.* Above right, *Pueblo designs painted on an arched gat with hand-adzed posts and lintel, Taos.* Left, *old gate with a simple cutout decoration, Santa Fe.*

ove, serpentine design surrounding an open panel with decorated slats, Coronado State Monument. **Below,** *three-paneled gate with painted chrome figures reminiscent of Navajo ritual sand-painting figures, Taos.*

149

Above, *carved roadrunner topping decorative wooden grillwork and handwrought hinges, Taos.* Below, *gate of rough-cut lumber and simple chip-carved zigzag slats, Albuquerque.*

Opposite page: above left, *old gate with cutout designs, the bottom section appearing to have been added at a later time, Santa F* above right, *modern gate with simple cutouts creating dramatic shadow effects, Albuquerque;* below left, *small cutout gate, Santa F* below right, *picket gate made with incised and painted slats, The Bishop's Lodge, Santa Fe.*

Top left, *a recent gate with zigzag splats and carved rosettes combined within a frame-and-panel design, Santa Fe.*
Above, *a contemporary gate utilizing traditional zigzag and cruciform shapes framed by a simple bullet carving, Santa Fe.*
Left, *a wooden gate with turned spindles and deeply carved shell crescents, Santa Fe.*

Opposite page, Top left, *old frame-paneled gate typical of Mexican construction techniques, Santa Fe.* Top right, *a frame-and-paneled gate with matching turned spindles in the transom, Santa Fe.* Bottom left, *a recent paneled gate with cutout cruciform decoration framed with coyote-style fencing, Santa Fe.* Bottom right, *traditional-style gate with both cutout and turned design elements topped by a carved shell motif, Santa Fe.*

152

Top left, *a restored paneled driveway gate topped with hand-cut crests, Santa Fe.* Top right, *richly carved gate flanked by carved spiral columns set in an adobe arch, Taos.* Above, *an old gate utilizing frame-panel design with traditional cutouts in two panels, Santa Fe.*

Opposite page, Top left, *contemporary gate with applied mitered designs incorporating a mail slot, Santa Fe.* Top right, *a hand-forged iron gate utilizing S and C scroll shapes with decorative flowers. This gate, possibly of Italian origin, was imported to Santa Fe in the 1920s, Santa Fe.* Bottom left, *restored paneled gate topped with hand-cut splats, Santa Fe.* Bottom right, *an antique colonial paneled gate with pintle hinges and interesting chip and carved designs, Santa Fe.*

Old New Mexican Dutch door showing a unique cutout design of hand-carved and chamfered slats, Santa Fe.

Contemporary metal gate of interesting design, Santa Fe.

Above left, *old wrought-iron gate with delicate cresting and design details, Pojoaque.* **Above right,** *iron gate with floral design, Santa Fe.* **Left,** *modern iron gate with diamond pattern, Taos.*

Above, *detail of a double iron gate with cutout cresting, Santa Fe.*
Above right, *old handmade iron gate with scroll and floral designs,*
Santa Fe. Below right, *detail of gate above right, showing collared*
construction.

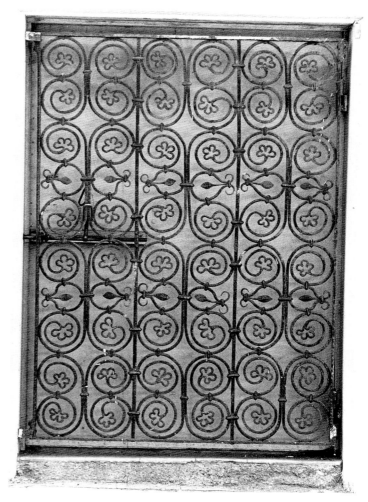

159

Above, *large double gate with lightning motif, Las Vegas.* **Left,** *double gate with triangular cutouts in mortise and tenon frame, San Ildefonso Pueblo.*

Opposite page, *vertical boards forming the background for a geometric pattern of applied rails, stiles, and panels on double gate, Santa Fe.*

Above, *one half of a driveway gate made of diagonal boards, zigzag grillwork, and large wrought-iron hinges, Taos.* Middle, *driveway gate with attractive cutout slats and an unequal opening.* Below, *plywood-backed driveway gate with decoratively applied solid wood panels, Santa Fe.*

Opposite page: above, *modern driveway gate with a painted Pueblo design, Nambe Pueblo;* middle, *driveway gate of linear Territorial style, accented by a hand-carved and hand-painted shell design, Tesuque;* below, *unusual driveway gate with V-cut pickets or rails, Taos.*

Opposite page: above, *old zaguán gate decorated with large iron* *bosses, the pedestrian gate opening on the left, Taos;* below, *modern* *adaptation of the zaguán gate, Santa Fe.*

Above, *zaguán gate with raised iron bosses and hand-forged corner* *braces, Santa Fe.* Right, *old zaguán gate with cut-in mailbox and* *decorative bird, Santa Fe.*

About the Author

Nancy Hunter Warren studied anthropology and art at the University of Delaware, moved to New Mexico in 1972, and has worked for the Museum of New Mexico Laboratory of Anthropology in Santa Fe since 1974. She has been making photographs for twenty-five years and has been published widely in magazines and exhibited nationally. She is the author of *Hispanic Villages of New Mexico*. Her photographs are included in numerous publications, among them *Christian Images in Hispanic New Mexico*, *Southwestern Culture History: Collected Papers in Honor of Albert Schroeder*, and *Maria Martinez: Five Generations of Potter*. She is a member of the Spanish Colonial Arts Society and a past board member.